THE RING

Also by Lynne Hjelmgaard

Distance Through the Water (I Want Press, France, 2002)
Manhattan Sonnets (Redbeck Press, 2003)

The Ring

LYNNE HJELMGAARD

Shearsman Books
Exeter

First published in the United Kingdom in 2011 by
Shearsman Books
58 Velwell Road
Exeter EX4 4LD

http://www.shearsman.com/

ISBN 978-1-84861-147-4

Acknowledgements

Four of the poems in *The Ring* first appeared in my earlier book
Manhattan Sonnets, (Redbeck Press, 2003). Others have appeared or are
forthcoming in *Acumen, Leviathan Quarterly, Poetry News, Poetry Wales,
The Interpreter's House, Jacket* and *Shearsman*.
A few lines I have taken from a poem by the Swedish poet
Gunnar Ekelöf (1907–1968). These lines I have placed in italics.

I would also like to thank Alice Notley and Dannie Abse
for their interest and helpful suggestions.

Contents

4. Paris

I.M. of Stig

For Stig

How I admire
you who moved
steadfast between countries,
even when there were deserts
to be crossed by foot,
oceans to navigate
by stars,
strangers to trust,
bargains to be made
with the gods.

(I become easily unravelled.)

You could get on a train
going in the wrong direction
and not panic.

And robbed
of everything
(as I am now)
and still
you found your way.

Copenhagen

You have been gone from the harbour almost a year

The howl in the rigging is louder.
Our best friend says you will come for me one day
rejuvenated from weathering your last Atlantic storm.
He still paints the sky and sea.

I stare at a flame and in an instant your body reappears as whole.
Denmark is good that way.
It wins competitions for the world's happiest population.
I can tell by the mentality on the bike paths:
all are equal until one disturbs a real speeder
or suddenly stops without making a hand signal
or rides on the sidewalk or crosses on a red light,
doesn't respect pedestrians or people boarding a bus.

It is important to follow the rules, keep up with traffic or step
        aside.
(Remember to keep the green buoys to port as you return.)

Sometimes it is harder now than at the beginning,
but our painter friend says you are busy sailing the waves.

Perhaps you can smell land by now.
(Though you love it best far from shore.)

I hope there is enough wind.
The seas wild and churning
I wait for you.
I see the sails filled and flying.

When we first met

You brought woven saddle bags from Afghanistan
containing: one pair of pants, a toothbrush,
two hard bound diaries with pages coming out and one pair of
        underwear.
There was an Afghan coat you sold in the desert
and the dirty pots you threw out of your kitchen window.
(They were too hard to clean.)
There was the return trip from Israel
with stuff taped to your body underneath your clothes;
and Jørgen who dropped a chunk in the airport bathroom
and you had to eat it and there was enough money for a taxi
from Copenhagen to Helsingør to see the sunrise when you
        got back.

You told me.
You dazzled me.
You gave me your ring.
Your foreign accent, then very foreign.

Now you call me love and I love to hear you say that.
And it feels like it comes from that space right below the throat
and close to the chest.
I don't want it to end though sometimes it seems
like we're on the way to already finished.
Our belonging, was it stronger at the beginning?
Will it be that at the ending? Is there a middle of the way
in between like the morning yesterday?
It seemed like you wanted me to walk with you to say goodbye.
I didn't know it until after and then I wanted to.
I would be silly to just run after you so I picked up your clothes
        instead.

At times I don't know where you're heading
but I wish you (me) were going back.
I'm afraid to look at you (me) going ahead.
Then you say you are a loner, I am your only friend
and you need to get a haircut tomorrow.

Where a rose has left you wounded

spring brings me deep
into the blossoming forest
where your tulips grow

a hawk chases a gull or swallow
shrieks, cries of other birds
behind the shadow
of a yew hedge

a tiny belly pants with breath
its twisted beak and flat wings
crushed on the dusty ground

the night isn't finished
I guide you back to bed

*

the easiest path
to the sea
is through the wild roses
the peeling lounge chairs
on the terrace, lavender
where the deer sleeps
in the morning

headless tulips
a smell of soap
on the body

afterwards, no longer you
alive there——

Your dinner spread among the universe

Your dinner spread among the universe. Can no longer taste.
Afraid of faltering, absorbed in sterile rooms. Drive me the
miles back to your bed.

It roars. Go back, go back the roar, we can't find cures written
on our thinning walls. Tired hands keep calling you down. We
aren't finished. *Wake me to sleep in you.*

Those who have received and been given, we can see it on their
mouth and eyes. I want you to see it on my mouth and eyes.

That was yesterday when dreams walked us around the house.
We spent the day thinking about porcelain instead of disease, if
it will release you.

The doe is lost in the forest. Large brown eyes alert, limbs
ready to jump. "Come with me." The immeasurable distance to
where you stand.

Vampiressa

I left you to wander the canal.
Let you have your fling.
I had mine with the village:

the endless hill, cafes, shops,
zebra crossings, all familiar.
When I returned you stood closer to her.

Her one sharp tooth, the black dress,
the pointed collar and sleeves.
Are you the one I've always known?

Now I turn my pillow
to face the sliced moon.

Copenhagen Widow

1

You shall not think that you are special.

Join a group.

Do not raise your voice in public.

Do not visit the Little Mermaid
(She's in China).

You can burn a Witch
on the longest day.
(If you dare get close to the fire.)

Kaerlig Hilsen, *with love,* (signed
the world's happiest population.)

(Your life costs the state *more*
than you can ever give back.)

Love thy neighbour . . . cautiously

2

Watch the moonrise over Carlsberg sign.
It could be Manhattan.
(The night we met.)

In time of sorrow, be a Viking.
Dry, salty, proud.

How to be happy again?
Pull up your socks.

Replace the tulips, the sheets, the bed.
(He would want you to.)

Will his Denmark be mine, not be mine, be mine?

Take a walk.
(Oh those hairy legs on bikes.)

Get out of your monkey mind.
Eat a pastry with cream and jam, read the paper.
(The way we used to on leisurely Sunday mornings.)

There are bonfires in the parks
and on the beaches
(where I thought I saw him gather wood.)

Remember to look where
the sky and sea merge,

as we did at the blue hour, twilight,
Our blue.

An Hour and a Half from Copenhagen

Two fir trees stand bare
melancholy but warm.

I flattened the sea grass
so he could make his way home.

He wanted his ashes
among the flying sands.
Those dunes close to water.

He liked trees with spines
of bald teeth and the smell
of burnt nettles, pine needles,
thistles, burr.

Our house was quiet.
Chickens cackled.
Rain pounded the roof.

The dead we don't know
are alive
at the entrance
where the crow drinks.

The Burial

You'd have left the gathering early
walked down to the edge of the garden
close to the waterline, puffing
your pipe, to wait for the rising moon.

The men talked: politics football vacations.
The women: babies jobs household products.
The new owners are redoing the house.
(Would you know it, outside or in?)

You are here with me again. I sit
in your chair or build a fire. I touch
your Christmas cactus, put my fingers
on its prickly skin.(Would you know me now?)

I look for us everywhere. My small hurts
that seem so trivial I could only
reveal to you. If I ask a question
with my right hand will you answer me

with my left? Your long ago words and
mine are embedded in our bodies. And
though you can no longer hear them I do
and will not leave you behind. Even as

I stare into dead nothingness, mutely walk
down to the edge of the garden, close to
the water nearer to you. A moon rise.
Between us no buried words to be said.

I give you a sea wind dried

I give you a sea wind dried sheet to smell
the ocean has you now
           here, breathe how liquid the spring

yellow blossoms used to be our craving
the mouth of a daisy's centre
           couldn't tell us,

we went with it
yelled and laughed in its halls;
           despite the fading

petals a tulip carcass is
open to the fullest, remaining leaves
           consoled by drink

and air, determined to be reborn
they won't give in
           their search invisible

nonsectarian, visibly soul
they are *nearer the hearth of birth*
           to you, beyond the flame

Its beautiful fury

Its beautiful fury brutally circulates
spring, high water marks the year
      this tide is in

our hideaway tempts me
to return as your secret witness
'where do you
      have him now?'

I point to my chest, the day
we went through pills
      to work through muscle, bone

and blood, the moon, still covered and
shouting *Light my*
      dead stars nearer you
images have finally stopped

the loosening up
of layer upon layer, the ball of
      sorrow, the person underneath

Tulip Lament

isn't it just like me to think something wrong
then I remember you were

in Denmark hanging laundry up
I hear your clogs in the hall

the deer are eating the tulips
and there is no one
to feed the birds

Go with all your ghosts
they wait in familiar places

among rosehips, clusters of reeds
the summer inside a sea
that didn't know

what the petals of a tulip
could contain:

that yellows die
tight lipped

that reds lower themselves
before the others

into little pockets
of their own quiet design

Two Songs

'Where you will next be there's no knowing'
                              Thomas Hardy

How did I know you'd give me
silver, amber and tulips?

Thunder comes unexpectedly.
The rumbling can stay for years.

Now that you are no longer
where do they go to the days?

Inside the house no rest to find.

The deer still sleeps on the terrace.
He eats the flowers.

How did I know you'd give me
silver, amber and tulips?

The Wave

I hear it coming.
It stinks of fish.

There are slippery scales and fins,
broken teeth and bones, jelly gobs,
rotten seaweed in mounds.
It covers the stones on the lawn,
the lavender and the heather.

The young birch survives.
So do my white Tibetan pearls.
Your Japanese grass.

I hear it coming.
It reaches the room that hears our words.

I wake up dry and thirsty for you.

Your History of Denmark

The stroke of your hand   left
                    traces of my girlhood
lying in familiar rooms
                    now disguised, now shady

through which my sister appeared determined to speak
You were in a state, not that state
                              and I
watched us from
above
      below
            within
another crash, just before the crush
            volatile brick by spitting brick
the   last   spiralled   stair welled   second

though
I, survived
(Touching my
chest
first hot/cold/wet
you
raised
a leg then
left/right/left
before the
settling.)

after you died I searched for your death
weeping   in shimmering black satin

my middle aged womanhood   held your Danish History part 2
      but

      we couldn't find a room
             near the middle of town
                    and your tongue

(I remember too much tongue.)

London

Things to do in London
After Ted Berrigan

Imagine London as a mountain with no top.
Climb.
Au revoir Copenhagen!

It's inevitable.
The Americans have met.

Where ya from?
No kidding.

Pretend to be French.

Think Wimbledon. Thud. Thud.
15 Love. Wow sunshine!

Attend local poetic events.
Schmooze incessantly.

Decide not to need anyone.
Lie.

E-mail Copenhagen, Paris, Rome, New York:
Hello!
I'm in London.

Wake up: strange
displaced, at home.

Is it Love?
Make it yours, your home.

More your home.
Become a London-er.

Walk towards them, loving them.

A long-lashed high-heeled jacket potato-ed two for a fiver pillar
box park-able right in front of your door London-er.

. . . nothing but some colors
sprayed into air and staying there
                    —Jules Olitshi

Pinked at the Tate

It's a jolly pink balloon
blown up to giant
with mesh fence around it
it's a bald headed
marshmallow with pimples
it's part of a chain store

It has one hand extended
(trying to give me flyers)
long and slimy like a lizard
another leg extended
back to ballerina stance
it whines too much pink
Wait Stay Shop

To get to the next floor
go down then
up the escalator
the woman ahead
has conspicuously pink legs

We are shadows of selves walled
moving upwards
pink collage stucco
position your feet
hands on your waist
head up back straight

a painting can
hold you there

It's pink!

I am pink above
I am pink below

I am musk of a rose
surrendered to being pink

Dog Dream/The Sunday Times

25 million in Russia are homeless
In U K both sexes prefer pretty Boy look
Pit Bull killed after attack
Somebody famous & contemptuous
Read poem in voice of Donald Duck
About Warsaw Jews with lots of W's and spit
(He was and is contemptible)

I dreamt there were dogs in hallway that wouldn't leave
That all crops, bridges, cities, trains
were covered by water except a few boats
At South Bank I jumped on freighter to North Pole
Saw lights of ships collide on ice
Heard lady upstairs drilling
went to bathroom, caught her in ceiling, made her stop

(I will get a Meg Ryan haircut
I will go to a silly movie at the Everyman
I will read A.R. Ammons' poems of Worldly Hopes
while eating homemade matzo ball soup
I will go to Tibet & meet the Dalai Lama
I will go on loving the man I love
I won't forgive everyone I've hated)

Weekends Away

1

The Farm

Waking up to a sticking-out horse head happily.
The closeness of his animal body, the neighing and whole
brown beauty of him framed against the barn yard wall.
I can not tell you the colour of his eyes and when I do think
shepherd he is but a vague shadow beneath a darkened
window standing guard beside his bizarre dog. (One time it
barked at my open door and cowered before me in a
submissive pose). The farm's owners are active participants.
She has her ponies, he has the town hall. Yesterday's
dilemma was water. Village currents turn between bliss-
fully peaceful (the chapel's graveyard, church on Sundays, teas
with the postman) and edgy discomfort (the demonic
thatched cottage which once locked me in its bathroom. I pounded
and pounded until released by my husband who was in
the front yard smoking a cigar). I am a tentative
guest. This hamlet, inhale it, forgive it its bleakness. The Village
Green-from there I heard a loud humming past midnight. I am
sure a lamb can be many things. (A llama with a bad
back, a goat with black ears, a hairless dog in heat). We're on
the lookout for sheep heads stuck in barbed wire. Will they stay
there 'til they die? They part like a river when we cross the
fields. A chequerboard patch-one brown, one harvested, one
dark green. Cypress trees line the road backed by hills. Chiming
        bells
are soft enough to be heard and fade step by step. I hear
galloping hooves, no destination, running manically
back and forth. Oh I fit wonderfully into this frame.

2

Aberystwyth

What most reminds of you?
An unsettled bay, an escalating wind,
a sail being hoisted.

*

Mist conceals a single spire
the castle, pub lights, student
bars as seen from above
hug the town.
A black crow caws

from hilltop to hilltop:
—you are no longer—
over wet chimneys
slate roofs and heavy walls,
filled and laid by hand.
Welsh stone upon stone

marks the tempestuous bay.
The Green Belt stretches,
a garden of raspberry bushes,
fists of pears and apples.
Lovely is the chill

where there is also warmth.
And though my hands freeze over
I would want you to feel

light shivering through windows
a new autumn open

and crackling like a fire.
I try not think about
bats under the beams,
hidden burial grounds,
or the river
at its full height and power
that carried you away.

3

Bunny

Your mother is lying on the road.
Each day she blends more
into the tar and pavement.
Pieces of her fur in the rubber of tyres,
on the bottom of shoes,
scattered on the banks of the Avon.
You scamper about on the lawn,
ignoring the lettuce, chewing the
same anonymous weed.
I imagine holding you in my palm
what would you do?
Quiver, shake, wiggle your nose,
chew my fingers, jump off and away,
Back to the wilds of Luddington,
White button tail, long ears, tiny head.

It is possible to taste in a dream.
I ate a rabbit, acquired its memory.

Rome

Things to do in Rome

Roll up the curtain
in your room.
Kill the scorpion.

Complain about the heat.
(Everyone does except the lovers.)
The forecast is steamy.

Walk until tiredness and
hunger overwhelm you.

Find the perfect shady bench
in the Villa Borghese
between the busts of Francesco de Sanctis
and G. Battista Grassi.

Rejoice with the first bite
of a tomato bruschetta.

Stare into space.
(*Where is he whom I love?*)
A chestnut may fall on your head.

Stretch on the grass.
(Like the priest in black robes.)

(Italians are good at petting
and praying in public.)
Be Roman.
Don't think so much.

Put feet in cool fountain
while reading 'Rough Guide
to Living . . .' (without him.)

Sleep in the afternoon when the breeze
comes up, Sirocco. You were the pinions.
He is the wind.

Who brought me to this place?

Disappear into the park
early, after a sleepless night

in the toilet the smiling Signora, *Gracia*

is black, white and red *tiramisu*
is cypress trees at the top of the stairs

a man sings his a's, e's and o's
everyone needs Borghese

the poets the ballerina the man reading his paper
the actors the parakeets the painter
who paints the scene of this poem

as magnolia
as conversation
as a grieving angel writes
on Lord Byron's face

'there is that within me which shall'

as young as old
as already gone

after forty nine days the soul
leaves the first place of light

cicadas take the lead
followed by swallows tweet-ing
geese cackling

the baby bird turns to dust
David fights the lion
Hadrian builds Antinopolis
for the boy who fell into the Nile

the first year it throbs
then numbs out
to less, moves
up through the throat
shortens the breath

to move in waves the way
the world does
when someone says your name

Villa Borghese

This is the afternoon of running water,
the scent of urine, coral beneath an archway
covered in soot.

A man lame and blind begs in the hot sun.
Yes, this is his afternoon
of cicadas, and a popping cork;

of tourists wading in fountains-
his sudden cry, wailing arms, steaming
hill, heat,
his torn pants his no teeth his one finger raised.

I fall flat on my face,
dirt in my mouth.
Thou art in the garden of the world.

We are all mere feathers in mud,
headless statues.

A water jet glistens
out of a mask
to the brim of marble bubbling.

Near Tempio di Esculapio

Every day there are seven new directions to take.
A tram, a hill, a road to anywhere to think about and
find my way back from.

Time in the garden spent circling, unknowingly,
the temple, the lake, for you

in Villa Borghese
with the poets at the gates,
with the perfume of the ground after watering,
with the hissing cicadas, the chattering tourists,
the cackling goose, the pinyon trees,
with the parts of you
I am hopeful to find.

You would have enjoyed
the elderly couple who rest in the shade,
the grandfather who pushes the baby carriage,
the man selling roses who comes around again and again,
the bus driver who stops the bus to drink from the fountain.

If taken from the right side of the Gorgon, the blood
was capable of bringing back the dead.

What does a cypress tree contain of secrets
besides burnt bark and claw marks
of an angel trying to escape stone?

Lost myself trying to track you down
Though you'll never be found
                              —Gomez

Falling City

Push with the help of heaven Cathedral
columns in patterns of marble swirl.

Inside: massive stone, from a distance whispers,
muted, muffled where eyes accustomed to dark
seek circles of light.

Will you appear out of the shadows:
your thirst quenched, hunger restored,
flesh once again flesh?

Life smells like yeast, and of wine spoiling
in ancient jugs. Bats circle the tower
but find no place to rest.

Madonna on top of the cliff protects the territory.
A mask with braided hair, a fixed grin.

At Campi d'fiori

(talking to Giordano Bruno)

you stand in the square, silent and hooded
knowing what we the lively don't

the life of a Roman seagull drips
down your back, cries at dawn

a woman is sitting at your feet
as if to embrace them

smile at the camera
the whole sienna square

(where you burnt at the stake)

I see you alive on the grass
in the Borghese, eating gelato, talking

rapidly to your students with your hands
wandering the streets of a foreign city

stroking your moustache, how different
you look with shoes on

Stay out of their Churches
Do not go back to Rome

they don't want to hear about:
the stars, the moon or the sun

(your tongue imprisoned because of wicked words)
your ashes not of a heretic or a saint

thrown in the Tiber

Song

Montale writes of his dear little insect Mosca.
How happy he sounds.

A baboon swings from the highest pole in the zoo and sings.

Even the woman who shakes her blanket from the window
next to the crematorium—

Laugh, a baboon.

When the wave washes over the house
the children become quiet and listen.

On the beach are old letters, history books, picture frames,
vases and paintings, your mother's plate.

What to do with the wash, the salt, the sea, the dead fish?
Take me warmer, take me nearer you—

Janus as ending sees the urn buried in the snow.
Janus as beginning sees the milk

flow to little Mia and
watches her brother dance.

Mosquito in a Roman Hotel

My adopted insect. With so much death
in the world I hesitate to crush you.

(A poet I read recently cannot
bring himself to kill any living thing.)

Poetry at its peak glorifies the All in flight.
Could it be the muse has left, departed

into the Borghese with the joggers,
the sweat, the cicadas ancient song?

I sit at the desk staring at my failed lines.
While you, little Italian, are just like

your compatriots. (I hear them still).
They move, talk and zing rapidly always

with emotion. You inch your way along
the wall performing evocative

Latino movements with your hind legs.
Planning an assault for the wee hours?

(A stomach bug from the Hostaria
is already attacking me from inside.)

In one second it could be over for both of us.
Whack! But you've found a mate. You soar. She hangs

on for the ride, buzzing *amore* as you descend
to this page, coupling in various positions.

I almost envy their lustful togetherness.
Two lovers wait to suck the blood from my words.

Weekends Away

The Elevator

The steep road is supposed to flatten out but it doesn't where
you think it should.

You pray it will get better but it only gets worse and hold your
breath and don't look down. The whole incline ends in one
soaring gull-cry sound.

Almost 85 degrees and up around the bend, the next one is
higher. The toughest climb is on the jagged surface of dust, dirt
and pebbles.

You heard a woman and her two kids got caught in her jeep,
she backed up too far and hung off the cliff. They were rescued
by her mobile phone.

You see a speck in the water that is the boat called Star Lady.
You are burning up.

You pray the hill will flatten out—only it gets steeper.
You think the jeep won't make it—it doesn't.

You end up out of the jeep on all fours doing a baby crawl on
        hot tar.
You watch it roll down the hill and wave goodbye.

You lift your scraped knees and close your eyes.
You cry when you get to the next uphill curve.

There is no way off the road but to crawl backwards.
There is a jagged surface of dust, dirt and pebbles.

The Locals call it *ascensore*.
Hold your breath and don't look down.

It's a turning point.
It's almost a sound.

A woman hung off the cliff in her Jeep; her kids were in the back.
They were rescued by her mobile phone.

Your ears pop, your stomach drops. What your head thinks is the
end isn't.
It swings you in a swirling S. The next peak is steeper.

Trouble is another bend and another one.
Electric wires over your head, the ugly water tank,

the lady hanging off the cliff in her jeep with her kids in the back,
the whining goats butchered into meat on the hill.

Satyrs, churches, monuments & ruins . . .

Closer to him
he is not a man
VITAE LAVDEM
but hooves tail curly fur
discreetly placed
horns.

Is he stealing her child
who rests between them
on their forearms?
His back bent, limbs fend
her efforts in a half-
hold half-pull.

Oh the strain of them, as long
and as much as they can bear,
inside bronze.

And we, placed around a centre
of what lives here, move in
move through them
know the struggle well.

*

Nuns sing behind a gate
arrange flowers whisper
on the altar.

Rhythms of breathing
where we meet the dead.
Do they love each other?

Words written in the form of a cross:
Seeking me in prayer beware of hurtful things.

The mask is eyes
nose and wreath.
The mask is
broken nose, cracked chin, beard.

The child caught by the tide
returns again.

A church under a city
a city under a church
they dig out all the dirt:
pieces of vast grotesque heads
interior carvings
busts placed in walls
mouldy chambers
from which appear
family dwellings shops
deep underground wells
pottery an iron grill.

What I think are Popes
standing on rooftops
are chimneys, a fountain

is a stream, a Golden
Madonna is carried by ten men.

*

In the mountain pass
cicadas' hissing
fills the open space,
here we can breathe.

At the grave
of the baby bird I lift
the concrete slab.

There is no quivering belly
crushed beak, twisted neck
flattened wings. Only dust.

*

In a blur of bubbles and pools
a small fish devours a large
dead one.

Whatever is in the bottle
the Satyrs want it.
It is a body part.

I can hang up a plastic heart
lungs or stomach
at home to heal *before*

you introduce yourself
as dead
to the Carabinieri.

Paris

Things to do in Paris

Go back
to get in touch
with familiar street smells:
the bread, moist
fruit, him.

Say Goodbye
at the top of the Eiffel Tower.
(Closer to where he is now?)

Find a place that sings. Sing.
(Don't know if you have tried this,
but would like to . . .)

In the cafe the Frenchman smothers
his girlfriend with kisses.
(Her head's on his lap.)

Find a lap.
(How would it feel?)

Think of Blvd. St. Germain:
the Italian, his earring, unshaven face,
limoncello, smiles rushing at you.

(Ex-cusee, ex-cusee.)
Befriend a few American writers.
You're travelling alone?

Eat Quiche.
Get a life.
Get a life.

Changing Rooms

1

My neighbour in Paris wants to know
when I'm moving back to USA
like I'm supposed to go back to USA
    and be happy
When I lived there I wanted
to go somewhere else and be happy
like he will always be himself
in the world
Just different

2

I often change rooms around,
large rooms with sofas, chairs
lamps, beds, sheets
that seem so permanent
or search for transportation in cities
where it's difficult to connect
Sometimes don't recognize
what country this is
I indulge in foreignness
Can be overwhelmed by a cold
odd feeling, even in a familiar harbour

3

Here could be home as any place
I want to make phone calls

After a walk I return to a green room
I remember from somewhere else
because of the see-through curtains
and high elevated subway
sounding like the Bronx

4

Inside a vacant building
near the Champs de Mars
walking up a flight of stairs
enclosed by cool, curvy glass

Outside the moon is full and pale
encircled by blood colored rings
Luminous beams touch my feet
I curl up on a green lawn carpet
and grow hands and wings

5

During a fight
I almost threw a shoe at him
"She said that, you didn't tell me that"
I don't want to invite American tourists
I don't know to dinner
or discover Paris with them or
offer to iron a shirt anyway

Do I feel comfortable in this tight dress?
Pas du tout
Has my French improved
Un peu
I miss America
Jones Beach, New York deli pickles, a turkey sandwich on rye

6

The Buddha Tree is too short
next to Blaise Cendrars' poems
I go through my books like neighbourhoods
& rest in the leafy corners of their bindings
The sensation of having them near me
their smell and his

Weekend Away

Things to Do in Berlin

at the Ritz
his name is Barney
get a tattoo?
learn Japanese
find the way out
read the love parts
practice: Drücken Ziehen Drücken Ziehen Drücken Ziehen
eat a Betty Boop burger

*

(I want Paris back)
had wave dream again
except
engulfed in a drowning
fall into sea space
at will
not drowned

*

a man at the conference
sits across from me cool
in Gucci Armani with laptop
black leather bag

they are very sensitive here but any moment
the atmosphere will crack and we'll all turn into
man-eating critters with teeth

*

boys at the door
painted faces & bow ties
(one man actually falls asleep
stays away from the group
doesn't talk to anyone
he says the coffee is too strong)
a look alike Marlene Dietrich
is covered in black slinky
top hat and wiggling ass
the man at the bar
with the handle-bar moustache
hoop earring
and long shirt
out of trousers
cabaret style
says home is overrated
has never settled down
moves every two years

*

I want Paris back
I want grey dew & mist Sun King's castle Jardin anglais
I want sad with a bit of happy & happy with a bit of sad
I want to open a window, say cheese

the rocks on my desk speak nothing say a lot:
the sky is bluest on top of the low valley rock
widest where it hangs like a blanket
over the mountain range rock

Prediction:

that if you get off
at the next exit
it will take you
as far as the next one

that if you don't make it
you'll try again

that the one way
system smells like
New Jersey

there will be some confusion
about where you live

you will never have to
wear black heels again

you will go back to Berlin

The Ring

'Even as we get better
we say we never will'
    —Alice Notley

My sister says she cries for me everyday.

No longer a wife
still married.

His side of the bed.

The night he slipped away
I grabbed the top of his shoulders
felt the nook of his armpit.

Still warm.

Men choke back tears
women let them out.

Ghostlike versions of ourselves
fade into weeping walls.

I phone a widow friend.
We mingle with each other's dead.

'After a while there aren't as many calls'.

Another widow
(older than me)
cycles around Paris
in high heels, has a Cuban Tango partner
who comes up to her chin.

What do I want?

I have taken off my ring.

www.ingramcontent.com/pod-product-compliance
Lightning Source LLC
Chambersburg PA
CBHW031932080426
42734CB00007B/652